❧ Fortress

Also by Brenda Hillman

White Dress

Fortress

Brenda Hillman

Wesleyan University Press
Middletown, Connecticut

Some of the poems in this book were originally published in the following: *The American Poetry Review, Ironwood, The Missouri Review, Pequod, Ploughshares, Quarry West, Tar River Poetry Review, The Threepenny Review,* and *ZYZZYVA.*

"A Life of Action" is for Jean and Lori. "No Greener Pastures" is for Naomi.

The author is grateful to the National Endowment for the Arts for a fellowship, and to Bob Hass, Fran Lerner, Robert Pinsky, and Naomi Schwartz for their help with the manuscript.

All inquiries and permissions requests should be addressed to the Publisher, Wesleyan University Press, 110 Mt. Vernon Street, Middletown, Connecticut 06457

Library of Congress Cataloging-in-Publication Data
Hillman, Brenda.
   Fortress : [poems] / Brenda Hillman.
     p.   cm.
   ISBN 0-8195-2167-1   ISBN 0-8195-1168-4 (pbk.)
   I. Title.
PS3558.I4526F6   1989
811'.54—dc19   88-16972
                    CIP

Manufactured in the United States of America

FIRST EDITION

WESLEYAN POETRY

for Lenny

❧ Contents

I

A Life of Action

Gray this morning, pigeon-gray, governess-gray,
not military.
Wake hung over from last night's lecture;
the couple spoke of war, their faces glowing slightly.
Two women sat behind me, holding hands.
—I had forgotten what this was like, said one.
—How beautiful your hands are, said the other.

The child coughs all night.
I give her orange syrup
that sticks to her hair,
then look out at the coins of leaves and lamplight
on the stubbled street,

and sit within the gray
of not deciding how to use the time,
the gray between decision
and the first step.
Think of E. already up, jogging.
Summon courage, like a moving van.

Better to have lived a life of action
like the woman said.
Better to have waved from trains at the bourgeoisie
instead of thinking thinking thinking
with this mottled gull of irony
above my head,
cawing, garbage-mouthed;

better to have cured the fatal contagion
or smuggled the letter
than to sit like a sparrow among sparrows
trying to focus on a shaft of motes . . . .

Well! Begin the list for Thanksgiving,
begin the errands in the brain,
the small temporal negotiations:

go down to Young's,
start tossing things into the wire basket,
tell Jean "Happy Holidays,"
holding the pear in one hand,
the yam in the other—it is gray
with a simple point at both ends,
like a story—

I love the way she lifts
the clear sack onto the scales,
chatting as she presses the buttons of the register;

it rings behind the suit of armor:
Good Cheer! Good Cheer!
and things slide on the belt like days on the calendar:

bags of hard berries, blossoms and herbs,
the bird with its ankles clamped—
the chilly, plucked skin,
the cave to hold the bright, good-for-you parsley,
the crumpled bread
(and will our guest rage, again,
"No more poems about sunlight!")

Outside in the drizzle
the woman will ease her baby
into the carseat, pushing its stomach
to hitch the straps over the flesh.
Who will reward her infinite weariness?
Who will glorify her?
I will says the housewife rain.
I will says the comrade sparrow.

The Shulamite Girl

Return, return, O Shulamite, return
that we may look upon thee.
—Solomon's Song

The doctor with Lake Tahoe in his eyes
has charts of an outlined, white-space man
whose colored meridians strike
his insides like the arrows of St. Sebastian.
The large, cement-gray-suited woman
who has driven with her son
from Sacramento sits before the doctor
and says she's the wife of Solomon.
"I am the Shulamite Girl," she says.
"And not only that," lifting her voice
like a tin cup, "I know for a fact
I am the bride of Christ."

The doctor shifts his clipboard
to the other knee. His pale assistant
shoots some liquid into other liquid
with a hypodermic, trying not to listen.
"Twenty-four years ago,"
the Shulamite Girl goes on,
"they locked me in a little cell.
No one came except my son.
When I got out after a year
with those crazy people, I told them
I was still the Shulamite Girl
and they locked me up again."

The doctor has a mind like the wood floor.
Her voice makes sharp, irritating sounds
upon it. After a few more
sentences he focuses behind her:
the hundred little cloudy amber vials
surrounding them like well-wishers,

the rolltop desk heaped with disheveled files
of other schizophrenics;
he watches a private plane scrape
the green hills like a razor,
his eyes wander to the charts, the mauve drapes—
there is no remedy for the Shulamite Girl.

You hover at the brink of nonexistence
with your soul-destroying love,
recalling the trees of frankincense,
the poetry of spices: saffron, myrrh, and cinnamon;
and after you've cross-referenced everything—
mandrakes and the names of cities—
you're still in the service of some abstract king
and you say of yourself, I am a wall,
knowing that even wrong dreams
might bear some benefits; as he has two
armies, you have the aquamarine
canopy of your belief.

Scott on Flight 559

The Burbank evening hugs the little jet.
Commuters, standing on the rubber-padded stairs,
can look inside the engines and feel comforted,
seeing how sensual, full-lipped they are,
the metal daisies in each one,

then open the starved briefcases on their laps
and study graphs of annual reports . . . .
You're traveling alone, crying, trying to open
                              the tinfoiled peanuts;
I settle in next to you, and we are trapped
by the fat man in the aisle seat, who goes to sleep.

You live on Howard Street, and you are six.
Only staying with your dad three days.
I can't get you to say much more, but can
adjust the nozzle of the vent, tell you the female
silhouette—the cop-show target on the button—

is to call the nice lady if you are sick.
You look at me. Brown eyes
like river pebbles. You don't believe me,
open your mouth a bit: the serrated tip
of your first permanent tooth, coming in crooked.

In the safari fabric of your chair you squirm,
open the Chicklets, look at the emergency card—
a smiling woman slides from the crashed plane,
her dress not even wrinkled. At least
your tears have stopped. I try

to help you in the Berkeley way
to talk about your feelings
but it seems a load of crap up here.
You don't know me. You miss your mom.
You have a one-way ticket, paid with cash.

The pilot's voice comes on, announcing altitude.
I fumble with the *Redbook,* read the recipes;
the cart is coming up the aisle,
its bottles ringing like the bells
of an old sleigh horse;

you're looking at the other passengers,
the tops of heads, those bristly hills of straw . . . .
What's to be done for you? Is there nothing?
I can't think of a story,
or reassure you with maternal chatter,

can only keep you company an hour
and just out of Oakland point
to where our light projects a cone
of tiny ice-flecks, spinning,

like something at once being seen, and the gift
of sight. In the beautiful void
over the lighted wing,
those ice children seem alive, moving
with no purpose but to be separate.

Broken Dreams

Anaheim's one black swan can dive
through his image and stay down a long time.
The white swan waits for him like a stone question mark,

and the crowds cross over the drawbridge to the palace
between the bright banners, beneath the steel claw
that simulates closure

because they believe Sleeping Beauty sits up there
in her drug-state, forefinger poised above the spindle,
hearing the mooring voice of Malificent

and waiting to tour Los Angeles like a high thin cloud.

Hot, swollen feet. Thousands of them.
This morning in line I looked down at a woman's feet.
The poor feet, twisted nails untrimmed, a little polish
                                    clinging to them,
shoved into sandals, waiting for pleasure.
The woman wore towing-company overalls,
orange writing on the back.
My heart hurt, and I heard this snapping.

> "I don't want the public to see
> the real world they live in
> while they are in the park";

Walt Disney drags this sentence forward slowly
like the thick stallions pulling trolleys
in predestined tracks down Main Street . . . .

> The surface layer of the dream is hot.
> Beneath that, a cold band of sadness.
> Beneath that, very deep, a cold joy.
> You've had to break something open to find it.

They rose at dawn, and then they went for pancakes.
He eased himself from the plastic booth,
jingled the change in his Bermuda shorts

while she cleaned the curve of her plate with a fork
and released the weak smile, like a warning . . . .

Midmorning. Lean against
the rented stroller. Watch the perfect couple
on a date, taking each other's pictures, exchanging
                                                            services;
fate has made them halves of the same thing.

I envy the hyphen, the ampersand, whatever bargain
they've made for beauty:
the king's son crossing the throne for the casket,
the girl in the papers who said she would die
                                        for David Bowie;

back in the room you are making calls—
rippling click as the dial retracts
to no one—and you wait for sleep to come.

        The cogs engage, the cable pulls the dreamcart
                            through the chosen medium:
        sixteen poison apples and no prince!

        I only dread that this will not go on,
        no dear one waiting at the exit
        waving some small, personal thing . . . .

Penny arcade. Plug the nickels
into Esmerelda. The amethyst bobs on the headband,
the stucco hand selects a prophecy
and the old machine vomits this white card:

You have been working everyday, eating, drinking, sleeping,
a little work and a little leisure,
where do you think it all will end?

(Not bad, Esmerelda; almost Heideggerian.)

You have never adopted any plan
without shortly afterward discarding it.
Work, economize, save, and you will win great success.

One of your lucky numbers is eight.
Drop a nickel in slot
and I will tell you more.

> They helped the old man into the long blue boat
> beneath the spires, the topiary gardens;
> then, as if part of a burial routine,
>
> the relatives got into the boat beside him
> and entered the arch that was dark with singing . . . .
>
> Jung had a dream of carrying
> a tiny light a long way through fog.
> —Very fragile, but it was my only light, he said.

The young woman loved the Parrot Pierre;
I loved her happiness—she lost
herself in the invented tropics, the clattering totem poles,

and when her baby pulled Louisa's hair,
she took the baby's fingers into hers and gently
rubbed them, so the baby loved the No.

Pure being. She had a face
like Tuesday Weld, that falling
grace. I wanted to *be her*—

>Why is experience so long?
>hacking the present out of mine-shaft memory;
>
>it's not the present that is difficult,
>and the wrong links of the past can be excised;
>
>I only dread that this will not go on,
>walking in the square
>beneath the shallow window boxes, blood-drops
>>of the geraniums,
>
>>gas lamps lighting the tender faces,
>>the men that go before me with their little brooms.

The woman in the Citrus House, exhausted,
says this is her last time.
I suggest she go back to her hotel, have a drink, a swim.

Good idea, she says.

I stare at the back of her neck. Delicate hairs.
Print of her dress quite faded. Birds
or something. Ruffles creeping up around the freckles.

I can't stop thinking the word Flesh.
Flesh.

>The kids are dancing in the Tomorrowland Pavillion.
>People try to photograph the smeared
>delirium. Baby lights in the trees are coming on

and pretty soon, huge sequined Tinkerbell
will sail above us on her wire stem.

From the glass-nosed train I see
the broken submarines at port,
and I recall the plaster mermaids floating in the coral,

the fishgowns pulled above their sloping breasts,
the turned-up fifties hair, the grins
like anchors as they guarded Disney's treasure
                        heaped so uselessly down there.

All day I saw the rigid men
speaking into walkie-talkies and thought,
Something is wrong with my place, then thought,
                        Don't think that,

just think of the laser face
of the woman in the crystal ball,
how she is created from nothing but light,

and is meant for illusion —
speaking her gurgling speech
as if underwater, she speaks from another world

in which she was programmed
not to act but to delight —

and the hologram waltzers in the ballroom,
how like smoke they are in their circling,
so that riding along, you can see through them,

both with freedom and without it —
the unconscious mind —

I preferred the fake blue arras
to the sky, the fake fireflies in the bayou
where the diners watched the flat bateaux

lurch forward toward the pirates in the haunted grotto,
and the shooting of blanks from the galleon,
the orange foil rippling instead of the fire,

so when the panel closed us out of experience,
reality wore that same
sweet shabbiness;

it was never any deeper,
never less a replica than this.

Saguaro

Often visitors there, saddened
by lack of trees, go out
to a promontory.

Then, backed by the banded
sunset, the trail
of the Conquistadores,

the father puts on the camera,
the leather albatross,
and has the children

imitate saguaros. One
at a time they stand there smiling,
fingers up like the tines of a fork

while the stately saguaro
goes on being entered
by wrens, diseases, and sunlight.

The mother sits on a rock,
arms folded
across her breasts. To her

the cactus looks scared,
its needles
like hair in cartoons.

With its arms in preacher
or waltz position,
it gives the impression

of great effort
in every direction,
like the mother.

Thousands of these gray-green
cacti cross the valley:
nature repeating itself,

children repeating nature,
father repeating children
and mother watching.

Later, the children think
the cactus was moral,
had something to teach them,

some survival technique
or just regular beauty.
But what else could it do?

The only protection
against death
was to love solitude.

Amanuensis

Sometimes at dawn they'd send the carriage for me;
for hours I'd ride in its hollow clatter
with only the driver for company.
And since it wasn't possible to sleep
I'd lean against fragrant wood, or clear
the usual circle free of breath.
With the world thus peeled away—spikes of grass,
untended like a giant's hair over the vast
expanse of the moor—I'd sit so lightly
on the rusty springs I grew tired being the driven one;
and always the question, like a rimless wheel:
Why was I sent for?
There were the driver's boots below the seat,
the delicate whip dangling beside him,
torn shapes in a bramble, somehow orderly;
then he would miss. Make a wrong turn.
Driver! I'd call him, but he would not hear.
Again they had sent the deaf one!
Never mind. I wasn't meant to get there,
but to understand the failure of the carriage.
Hired to write things down for them,
I would begin: "The moth has eyes
on her back, and nervous ways,
she too is autumn's secretary."

Bookstore

We were clerks in a shop at the edge of America;
people would come by but they were mostly asleep,
even looking at the books they were asleep—

books on the *Book of the Dead*,
on reader response, on awakening—

and we would not wake them because they needed their sleep
so we stood very still and quiet as they passed;

but the thin black lines kept blurring on the order forms
we alphabetized as we talked to the people
and drank the cappuccino with its collar of foam.

They'd say the monarch butterflies were migrating again,
taking their Halloween capes to Monterey
while tourists stayed inside to watch the insects
                                        in their predicament,
turning the field glasses on their dark-veined wings;

the neo-Marxists came forward out of the sunlight, chattering,
they'd go in pairs,
in seedy sports jackets with tiny plaids,

they'd stand for a long time before the hike
into the hermeneutical air, a saffron glow rising
                                        from the theories
flattened, like the butterflies—

theories from France, theories with graphs and spaces,
living theories, festschrifts for the dead—

or whistling the Brandenburgs
they'd plod back to the shipping room;
not yet! we'd say, Another few weeks or so!

And they'd say O.K., I guess, disappointment mixed
with resignation, like the eyes of addicts on the avenue—

Rousseau's bastards,
those souls rough as saddle blankets.

Maybe they'd been drinking café au lait,
staring nervously at the descent of sugar in the glass,

like the lunatic who sucked his fingers in the corner,
or the blind one by the bank, shaking his box,

the one we called the czar's lost daughter
who had hyphens in her name,
bought boxed sets on the installment plan.

Sometimes, when we'd start the day's procedures—
metal clips, croissants, move the recalcitrant
                              dead bolt's internal arm—
there was a howler at the door,

so J. would go out as St. Francis, and say,
You'll have to go away, my friend, and the man would go away,
tipping his head like a spaniel.

Once I saw a kid stuff a book in his pants.
Broad stone face: an Easter Island statue.
He'd chosen a large book with maps,

and he trembled as he did it, like a revolutionary—
Why did I, grabbing it from him, think the book
felt like a baby as he ran,

that I who had seen was implicated?

Abject is the watcher.
Abject. Having no lamp,
you must not enter the churchyard . . . .

Always to be subjective, like a book,
that's what I wanted; to face inside,
but also to turn out, to have a soul that would resemble paper,

and be carried out into the alabaster street
where, on the other side of order,
there was no suffering . . . .

Friday afternoons in the pre-spring,
C. to the right in black and red, her legs tapping time
to the filament of jazz,

the fragments would blur together, and I was immensely
                                        comforted by this;
the customers would stare inside
as thought stares into meaning,
cupping their hands around their eyes,

the dime-sized relics of their breathing
on the glass, and the last of them
would enter, relinquishing their packs—

Help you with something? Not really. No.
They'd have some terrible title. The Female
Universe. The Natural History of the So-and-So.

Once I thought these books could talk,
that they would, some nights, fall down from shelves
                                        onto their spines,
and open up and read aloud to one another,

and all the cacophony of that shared reading
made one voice, the voice of huge blue unforgiving
knowledge that had judged my life.

At 4:00 P.M., the secretaries would start to go,
the mailman had been, eased the shipment from the dolly
                                        with his boot,
and we'd settle in;

a little rain had started,
the customers would put on their gear, hunching their
                                        shoulders
to bear up under historical time,

holding the books like infants under their arms
and we would stay on in this timelessness . . . .

The great desire had been to join them.
One step and we could join them but we would not
                                        take that step;

they were so much like us, taking into the scratched night
a few facts, and a longing which,
because it was so real, sustained the life.

No Greener Pastures

Under stress the great hawk circles,
holding greenness in its eye;
under stress the greenness travels; and under
stress the eye perceives this,
making chemicals to lift the spring;

but I have taught all morning
Hypothesis, Inductive Leap
until the mind had within it
no questions,
and no leaping,

though one kid has written, for my benefit,
"The hills have a certain
greenness about them." And another:
"Nature as a hole is beautiful . . . ."

Where is there a better place than this?
What we want is simply past our reach.
I drive back home through the beloved hills
and always the same image comes to me:
the sight of a Victorian lady
shifting under her coverlet,
the sense that beauty is too far away.

No one behind me now; I pull over,
the sleek white flanks of my Toyota glint in the mirror.
Half a mile from Inspiration Point, black loops:
the hawk circles the dead thing, like an English teacher.

An hour ago the students did the midterm,
produced the knotted writing
like saved string; I heard
the whispered thumping of a ballpoint
as it hit the page
inside the hamster cage of an Idea—

they looked up—something was missing!—I looked out

to the green hills, longing to be there,
and thought I saw, beneath the anorexic cross,
some crawling human speck,
the little pioneer!

Gold glints in vectors off the mission in the suburbs,
the Virgin implores in the alcove—
always the impediment here.
Always language first
and then the hills. The lover,
then the avatar. Shall we tell
the students *that?*
There's a gap between the spirit and the world
and nothing nothing
ever fills it up!

In 1962, on my mother's Remington,
I typed the novel, *No Greener Pastures.*
An earnest girl, full of ardor,
led the wagon train. Love came
and went like malaria;
there was a birth, a wedding, or a death on every page,

and how pleasantly disasters pressed up
through that blue typescript, single-spaced: snakebites
through muslin, the nightly circle
of disease and complaint—
but writing was like reaching
California—the absolute condition
with a beach—

I want her back, that sweet commuter.
She stayed in a shawl, chapter 16, eking out dialogue . . . .
The car coughs a little, loaded with essays.
I go the back way, turning out to rest
at the gritty, lovely U. My colleague
takes the brave route back to camp; after the meeting
I saw her clutch the wheel, and squint
before she drove onto the ramp, her immigrant
braids curved gracefully the way
she had to pull upward through the rather
meaningless arrows—

Cleave and Cleave

The lifeguards have gone in for the season;
their stilted chair
still looks out like an egret on the strip of sand
that's cluttered with artifacts: one thong,
sun-lotion bottles, the sunken
pockets of footsteps filled with trash.
I stop on the cliff and stare down at the lake
that builds its private character in the off-season,
imagine sunbathers skiing now,
taking their introverted goldenness
down the bright slopes.

In the parking lot,
a young couple embraces, coming from
the shoulders of the lawn with picnic remnants,
and finding their Buick he presses her against it
and she tilts her sun hat toward him so it
catches the light like a last
phase of the moon — she knew
it would do that —

The cold takes up this image
and shatters it; she stumbles, touches
his arm, buttons her top button
and for a second the absent bathers seem to come back,
surrounded by plastic shovels and towels,
and with bland curiosity, trying
to understand that this happiness
is not unlike their own.

Minutes later, another couple
comes out screaming from the shadows,
and running along a white line, he spins
her around: "Why don't you

say something to me, say something to me!"
They have driven a long way to fight in public;
the absent lifeguard is hurrying over,
the girl puts her fists over her eyes,
runs around the car like a flag
on the antenna,
just circles without form, but I keep
walking, so I don't know what will happen later.

Spinoza, who ground lenses, looked
past the bestial shapes of furniture,
past the powdered glass
to human nature
and believed every substance is infinite, but
love may be extreme, and the mind
distracted by this can ruin
the perfection of God;

and there are those
linguistic twins *cleave* and *cleave*,
which stem from opposites, meaning
split and stick, two same
sounds arriving like coincidence
in the day or in a breath:
I felt such freedom when you walked away;
I won't stop loving you, even in death.

❧ II

We had the kids and Anna with us. We all started off to a huge fortress where I thought we would be protected. As we were going, we entered a city. There was a church. The kids and Anna started up the stairs. "Come back," I said. "You have to stay with us. We all have to stay together." So we continued on our way to the fortress.

—from a dream

The Ropes

The ropes all night! The ropes
dragged me from sleep to the edge of the world,

slapping the window with their girlish braids,
but there was no girl,
only my familiars
in their dearest flutterings:
prison, racetrack, school
edged in red,
smoke from a freighter
blearing its thought behind
dawn's poor detail,
and the insect pathways of a military base.
Like water
in a sieve, the first birds came.
And still the ropes beat the side of the house—
not an unfriendly cadence finally,
in fact, nearly reassuring:
you have survived before,
you will survive this time
these gray imperfections,
until the sound joined every sound in the universe:
the foghorn that always calls the same child,

and the clamor of the great bell,
and the shaking of the mast as if the ship were real.

Fortress

1. Night Watchman

August, the season of mild excess,
and the moon comes out like a rumor;
the night watchman stands on the avenue,

weaponless,
kicking one low black shoe with the other
while people go in and out of the liquor store.

There is a row of bottles behind him like bowling pins,
a cashier smoking beside the jars of olives,
and a tall cardboard man in a tuxedo, holding a martini,

and colorful refrigerated items with halved, sweating fruit;

but the night watchman is sober and short,
his crooked badge has numbers and a floral wreath,

his whole body blocks the doorway
as he hums a greeting to the regulars
who have come out, in desperation, at midnight.

Hollow, aren't they, these short stretches
before the hours when we'll be given
so much weight from the world we cannot bear it;

so straight he stands in his ironed uniform
that we believe he believes
this life is not a sham, that he is at the fortress
                                    of an ancient city,

and as a few leather shadows pass
attached to no one, the watchman
checks his wrist and smiles and spits from his
                                    imagined parapet.

Fortune's slaves are bored tonight;
their houses glow like amber dice
from deep inside the universe.
A lady scratches at her payments.
The man above her types till dawn.
Blink goes the tower's dotted H outside the house,
the flash and scallop of the bridge.
Roar, the voices in the dungeon, on the phone
                                        to friends . . . .

Sometimes at night in the quiet you have seen
something like yourself among the captured things,
then said No No it's not me it's nothing,

nothing but the widowed evergreen
tangled in corduroy darkness . . . .

To live as if each hour were the last,
is that it? To love
the accidental midnight loneliness,

and love how the night goes on without you:
the radio tower, winking its ladder of blood—
secret, climbing sounds—

and past downtown, past Potrero,
rugs and bracelets of lights
spread out for insomniacs,

the free curl of factories and tracks
down the peninsula,
so much longed-for light that you beg

don't go yet night, stay longer, but it can't . . . .

And in the morning, when the gulls return
like the souls of the dead
over the landspit, the broken finger,

they are more beautiful than they might have been
had you not been so tired like this,
cloth decoy, greeting their Otherness

behind the rainy waters of the bay.

II. Types of Nothing

Mrs. H. cleans out her garage,
gathering refuse like a large mouse.
In autumn, she works for Queen Death, as I do,
pushing half-living things into the mouths
of slick, black sacks,
prodding the supplicants from their huddle
where life had resentfully thrived in the rot
and now rolls forth in little armored tanks.

Lieben und arbeiten. Love marries work.
Freud does not base his books
on Mrs. H.—gap-toothed, bent-over work
that slams the pasture gate of the soul
and twists exotica in the dirt—
he puts the stammering *lieben* at the center . . . .

She wears the same blue nightgown seven years,
lace drips around her ankles as she gets the paper,
stopping to tie the plackets
of the yucca; and later

walking her lame husband down the stairs
she almost lifts him into the Ford,
prepares to drive him to the Lake of Forgetting;
but first, she calls across the street to ask
in the last-leaf-on-the-tree tone of voice
if I know the schedule for the trash.

Are the colors of the body as true
as the flesh of sunsets?
I don't know. I've been reading a book about auras—

the lilac-blue of "higher spirituality,"
the orange of "pride"—
but nothing is as beautiful as the world outside:

Richmond, with its fringe of industry,
pastel oil-storage tanks like big vitamins,
the warehouses on the Point, canvas-white;

even Albany is better than auras—
hell-circles dimly laced around the Depressed Man
in Plate Sixteen,
the Angry Man's dazzling oval like a Russian Easter egg.

After a storm here there is such a shine off the water,
like the shield of a great warrior laid flat;
stupid Satan, offering to give the world away—

all this will be yours if you just bow down:
the train mending the landscape with its glass needle,
the left face of the bridge turned toward the sea,

the trucks along Route 80 like white grubs,
southbound to fruit country.

"Last night a running professor
stood next to me, trying not to eat.
Very skinny, his face a bit drawn.
Fear death by running.
He talked about the illness of his buddy,
nodding, punctuating pauses
with more nodding.
—If that doesn't work, they'll have to try blank.
The wine was so weak I could see to his shoes:
blurred, floating seeds.
Death-talk is not a type of nothing. It is solid."

　　　In autumn here, the bees explore
　　　the metal edges in their slippers,
　　　keeping the important powder on their legs;

　　　love is the type of nothing
　　　they use to forget who they are.
　　　Their plump mistress stirs in the corner,

　　　determined brilliance
　　　that drives them to risk.
　　　She will kill them if they keep up their sweeping;

　　　they must fly off somewhere without warning
　　　but they are dazed by this proud voice calling,
　　　and sick from this high, mild weather . . . .

　　　　There is a woman with a red face, walking,
　　　　there is a woman in a red coat, walking,
　　　　one glove in her upper pocket—
　　　　　　　　her breast is waving!

They've taken the larynx out of the dog
so he won't disturb the neighborhood.
But he still opens his soundless mouth, loving his own
                                        subjective barking.

Few natural noises here. The wet thwack
of the paper at 5:00 A.M. The foghorn's two-note
tired bass viol behind the fast entrance of the garbagemen;

and every morning, the favorite sounds:
the clatter of junk mail, paper on iron,
the helmeted sparrow's transcendent song;

I should love this, it won't last long,
the merciless whine of the saw,
the dry peck-peck of the typewriter bird.

And ah, suburban night, when these sounds cease!
When the M.'s boy is resting from his paper route,
and the bridge club is letting out,

and lying there I hear the street gossip as they hold
                                        the handles of their cars and talk,

and at midnight, the tiny chimes
of someone entering the temple, or the wind . . .

    My running partner, *persona unknowna*,
    chatters about her dissertation.
    We do the loop. At the rim of the park,
    six trees stand together,
    one stands apart.
    I love those seven trees so much
    I never want to visit them,

not admiring what they are
but the nothingness between them . . . .
Must think backward to the casserole:
Will the glass bowl do?
A horned owl sweeps by us—
the abyss has bushes! nocturnal feasts!
But the trees cannot support
the great yearnings we have for them,
nor the tower, from which the night subtracts,
as from a fevered patient, the heat
by inches, a pale calibration.

In December, when the rains come finally,
that first timid storm has the sound
of someone drumming lightly on the library table,

but later, not so soft and weak;
it mimics the hooves of an entourage,
it mimics the typewriter upstairs.

And like the daughter who's been asked to spin flax into gold
you think you ought to use the hard times,
take the flutter from the present tense, profit

from experience—why don't you forget it?

Outside, surveyors pound the stakes to take
                      the emptiness from California,
tying nasturtium flags to posts,
leering at distances;

important for you just to stay awake.
Turn on the little voice-defying fan—

the cat is learning how to crawl
through leaves the color of old fire
and make of them a dull, delicious bed.

III. Fortune's Slaves

a. Money

The bank tellers stand in their stalls
like the steeds of Hercules,
nameplates between them, partitions between the names—
mostly monosyllabic—
and black pens on their chains.
As they type my numbers in I make nice small talk
for fear the troll
will appear in green letters screaming,
This woman has no money, do not release her!
Louisa patiently spins the dial of the huge fake vault
for children;
a man behind us helps himself to free coffee
in a styrofoam cup
and sprinkles in two kinds of powder;
and we are released
to the flower shop: hyacinths in December,
yellow tulips forced from pots beside the plastic windmill.
This shopping center, my salvation.
Half of the wine merchant shows above the counter.
Smoky, excavated bottles in the drugstore.
The man who looks like a serf in the hardware,
ready to help me duplicate the key; and all I need
to get this help is
money.
Such a little thing so abstract so dirty.
Others who need it

come from the luminous mist;
one drops her bills into the mailbox,
that bold, accepting sentry.

b. Cocaine
One friend loves the little black angel,
one friend loves the dismal rain,
one friend laughs whenever I call her,
that's because she loves cocaine.

Pull the phone cord to the window. Don't waste time,
                                you can talk and think . . . .

Fog so thick surrounding the fortress;
will the courier get to us in this fearsome weather?

Behind the eucalyptus, the red-ringed moon
is being peeled back slowly, like the truth . . . .

c. Termites
I kick the wall where the termites are.
I read they like to groom one another,
like the ladies I saw in the nightclub bathroom,
fixing each other's hair.
The kings and queens have compound eyes
and frail, veined wings they lose after mating;
I find the wings on my windowsill.
Is the body hierarchical,
going up and down in the same life?
There is a caste of wingless workers also,
making their own fortress by subtraction,
and a caste more physical than physical:
pale, sexless soldiers that will plug
discovered damage with their heads.

d. Harmonica

Hi, said the street person.
Hi, I replied.
That your kid?
Yes, I said.
I don't hate kids, I use to be a kid, if you hate kids
    means you hate yourself (wah wah wah goes the
    harmonica).
He leaned forward at the metal table.
Close-cropped hair; tan and pink.
I took Louisa quickly away —
she was involved with her strawberry ice —
I kept looking back at him.
Not pity; there was simply no difference between us.

A few more skinny notes, and then
he covered his face with his hands.

e. Gold Tooth

Lately I can almost doze
beside the dentist's blood-flecked porcelain bowl,
watching the wind-up thrushes
in the ornamental cherry.
The dentist makes one molar pointed,
a little Himalaya,
his broad wrist turning the crooked mirror.

Then the dentist tells his story.
When he was shot down in World War II,
they took him in for questioning
and let him sleep on the stone floor;
all night in the unchallenged dark
a guard stood by him, and toward morning
put his overcoat around the sleeping man . . . .

What happens to your gold tooth when you die,
I ask him later.
They're supposed to leave it in, he says.
Something valuable because unrecognized,
like perfecting a small gesture,
or being a speechless exemplar of love;
the dentist paints the numb spot with some oil of clove.

f. Comfort
The print of the fortress by Lorenzetti
shows crumbling decadence;
moss has gotten to it
and some cardinal-red trouble off to the side,
but the fortress triumphs
over the bare ground, over the nameless sea

as one swift boat makes its way to the tower,
possibly with tea;

and in all the upright windows
and astigmatic doors,
long reclining shadows with specks of light,
so many ladies had been leaning out
and now step back to their weaving
under the dove-laden tiles,

back to the castle of comfort, to comfort the conqueror,
because all misery can be processed inside
if there is comfort and order . . . .

This morning I say good-bye to you,
holding the daffodil up like a torch.

IV. "Desire Which Springs from Sorrow"

The cashier at the Pussycat Theater
is propped in the glass booth,
her mouth next to the lead microphone,
her thick, half-finished novel on its face,
her head resting on her fist as she waits
for the man to come up with the change.
Ten A.M.; the little man
has come to see the movie of the ladies with whips,
followed by "Dormitory."
The cashier leans forward, whispers something.
What does she say? Does she see him every day?
I head down Telegraph.
Stretch pants in the window.
A woman pushing a door open with a grocery cart
while her kid bobs to some interior music.
When heading back at dusk I see
the cashier has gone,
there is a hole in the glass where her face was.

      Impassioned whispers, and nothing follows . . . .
      Through your ex-wife's binoculars
      I watch the wiglike, messy nest
      for movement, but really
      I can see without help
      the condominium she has devised
      of stiletto eucalyptus leaves,
      her pencil-yellow beak,
      the eye in profile
      black as a business phone.
      Hers is a California life.
      First she built the nest,

then she got married.
The father of the egg takes over sometimes
while she splits seeds on the patio,
her heart not really in it.
After a gentle rain, the nest disintegrates
but she still sits there;
over this plotless scene
I pass the double stare.
Maybe we'll find it later, down below,
a ring of mud and feathers,
the constraints that housed the miracle . . . .
Spring—delirium!
When lobelia are planted six inches apart,
when risk comes, like a squirrel on the wire,
and the robin, its bib stained like a waiter's;
and the descendant of the Transcendentalist
thins out his junipers
and totals his sycamore because
"I didn't like the leaves," he said.
Tree hatred.
The stunning acacia Mr. S. calls
"that weed."
The scarlet eucalyptus
the punk kid calls "testicle tree."
The apple producing its first poem.
The plum tree with its fate neurosis.
Spring: Last night at Cesar's,
the high-heeled woman
like a praying mantis—
delicate perfection—
her partner, programmed not to last,
knowing he's not good enough,
will never catch her
for she steps through invisible squares
to another world

and he tries to get there, pulling
himself to her skirt by the notes
of the flute
but she will make him disappear . . . .
Spring—a tulip moon.
Lilies like the hats
of two night nurses, whispering,
the scuffle down the corridor,
laughter that excludes you.
Spring. The man
who sold the place to us
raised rabbits down below.
Every March I watched the mama
pull her coat to make a nest.
Limpid pink eyes staring through me,
fat happiness, tearing its fur,
saying, "I am supposed to do this."
Spring.
My friend loves the little black angel
She doesn't want to have him,
just to watch him on the video,
twisting in his chain-mail suit.
Spring!
I see the silk threads
snails put upon the porch
and think how simply
all things leave themselves behind,
idea upon matter,
the shove along the ground
into the garden.
In the extreme
five-to-six before sundown,
we watch the hemlock:
great drooping arms,

the tender cinquecento sunlight from the side.
Through the window, a kettle screams,
the scream dies
as someone lifts it from the fire.
The hemlock, looking downhill,
shrugs off splendor.

v. The Last Days

August, the season of nothing doing.
A black dog paces in the yard next door,
parsnip-white paws stretched out before him—
he hates to sleep, and barks
his irritating, lonely, fierce, proprietary bark,
then shakes the petal caught between his teeth
from the rusty camelia he's eaten;
he's François Villon,

he's Richard II,
pacing between the eternity of chairs
next to the trellis of the couple
who is divorcing, waiting for his owner,
who has the night shift, to wake
beside the skewed Venetian blinds,
beside the green bottle on the window ledge
and begin the night, complaining and sleek . . . .

I peer through the iron bars
of the look-out door:
an evangelist, curved
as in a Christmas bulb.
He has knocked outside with a carpenter's force,
and starts his pitch, shows me
the disaster pamphlet, asks me
if his kid can use the toilet.

When the boy comes out,
he takes his place beside his father.
Duplicate suits. Serene faces,
white flowers above their heads
like flecks of ice.
These are the last days, he says.
I say I know and give him thirty-five cents.

You like the kind of diorama
in which one wall is taken away—
where you can see a gopher, hibernating,
or the anthill, sliced in half behind the glass—
because you had a castle like that once,
cross-sectioned, with gothic arches
out in front, where chinks of light
stood for the Middle Ages.

And you could do the whole routine:
a man pulling a bucket up a wellhead,
ladies at their vespers, people eating
at the trestle table on plates made out of bread,
and bleary pigeons roosting in the gutters,
hired watchmen pacing on the battlements,
folks with spears sleeping in the Great Hall
with warm orange straw spread about them . . . .

You could reach inside and make it work.
And when you had given them their places,
or when you had sent them all away,
was it enough to have love in your heart,
not just for the characters,
but for the hard arrangements
and the absolute freedom that kept you there?

After dinner, everyone played games.
Or minstrels would come forth and entertain them.
The lute player with the crosshatched sandals.
The hooded man with bells. The juggler.
Many of the party joined in singing,
and many watched from the stone bench
while the lady and the baron
did a halting dance.

"Night and Day"

In that famous misery, thinking she might join him,
he brought home instructions so they could practice;
he put the disk on and started shuffling,
with his hand on his stomach for a flat, imaginary wife;
and she sat nearby, in her bathrobe, watching
the way light struck his pants legs
in obtuse angles, dust motes
doubled over, scattered, like the stream
of urgent moments he had made his life.

Why had he brought the illustrations, she wondered.
He must have known she wouldn't dance —
not that she held out exactly, but in those times
(like the night the drunk man fell on her)
it was best to look as if you could, and didn't want to,
kicking your shoes off under the cocktail table
where they'd lie sharp-beaked on their sides.
He could have White-pants, queen of the dance floor,
under the strobe lights like ostrich skin —
or the one with the grin, whose brown flesh glowed
                              when he described her . . . .

Here in the living room, the business was different;
someday he might learn to let go in this,
someday he too might have pleasure.
She flattened the Xerox,
the ghostly footprints of the dancers on the page:
the lady's high heel, a triangle and a dot,
repeated like some terrible compulsion,
the man's lumpish-looking, inky steps — desolate doorways,
the ring of arrows swirling right out of them
into the deathy whirlpool of the mambo.

Only the tracks remained of this pair, as in an ancient site
where the people have fled from the unknown disaster.
The more she watched, the more satisfied he seemed,
seeking in his black thrall a certain perfection,
though as the evening passed he had no need of her,
for he had been joined by the notion of art.
Leave him alone! she shouted into the circle they made,
his beautiful art and his belief in its ruin;
leave him alone! she cried, It wasn't worth it!
But the couple continued to turn.

❧ III

Crooked Bridge

The light you love—the color of weak Scotch—breaks
sharply on the bridge this afternoon, perhaps
so the Sunday families can shout their nicknames
down a corridor of leaves, race their strollers
with a kind of tragic cheer, lose each other
briefly, and recover, and you who have come here
as your split self can make the important footsteps
both of the doctor and of the executioner.

You've brought the plastic sack
of bread—always the pretense of being
the provider—and hurl the torn squares over the rail
into the tangled moths, the notched
ferns pushed up from the Pre-Cambrian;
at once the ducks appear, a slight gurgling
in their throats, everything always and everywhere
depending on you, until you fail . . . .

But today an old couple stands beside you,
in loosely hanging cotton clothes, shouting
in another language, that urgency
because of death's warm muzzle on their shoulders;
not needing you,
they gesture in rage and terrible
affection into the tea-colored pond;

so you stand in the middle of the bridge as in
the middle of your life, alone,
until the ducks come in their preassembled
throng, Jewel Lake contained
and shining like Augustine's description of
the pagan world, the world
"with all its deep loves, with all its terrors,
with all its countless ways of going wrong."

Redwings

Something moves
in the Old Testament rushes.
I put the notebook down:
a redwing blackbird, crimson shoulders
dripping like the Red Cross pins
my father used to get for giving blood.

Summer afternoon; nothing required
but to watch Jewel Lake's clean
California scum, the army green still comforting
after ten years, the ducks, smooth
as wooden decoys of themselves;
then the old couple comes to sit.

"You know what is an angiogram?"
he starts right in, with the accent, bifocals
showing half of me and half of him.
"It's when they take a picture
of your blood. They put the tube up
under here" (reveals the delicate blue ankle vein);

"I told the nurse after so much pain,
Blessings in the name of Karl Marx!"
His lady friend laughs for him.
Good-natured fear, like you and me:
she's the shape his spirit takes
when it is free. A mother duck

parts the reeds like Cleopatra,
her double tail quotation marks into the air—
ripples of implication or a farther swim—
she has abandoned her children in the scratched
surface of the pond. Perhaps it's better to be
dependent, like a reed—Pan's girlfriend—he used

her hollowness to sing through;
the redwing goes from tree to tree, blood
on his wings, blood from the story, transcribing it
like a short secretary. The old man
watches this; his companion smoothes her skirt
to compensate for his elaborate innocence.

The Calf

The sun subtracted the ordinary
and left the russet hair
of my friend to lead the way;

we'd passed that family on the path,
the black bull
and the cow whose baby shied over.

There was a ring of time around the calf.
I could feel it:
a hard ring describing his fate,

the eyes like chestnuts
with a speck of shell peeled away.
We had the same talk every day:

sonata: the single theme which doubles,
and we'd be hurt
by what we couldn't say. We had just

done this when the baby left the mother.
We watched his mount-rushmore
skull from the side

as he focused
on the most desolate place
with the absolute attention of a lover,

climbing through blond, immediate grass
as a bad thought can climb,
from uselessness;

why didn't she notice? Shifting
her weight in the swamp,
moving the mud in her low area,

her stick legs holding the table
of her torso flat
because of the white patches

like spilled milk on her back—
why wouldn't she notice?
My friend whimpered;

the calf climbed over the hill
and was lost
while the cow held a sloppy sprig

of watercress in her mouth, eyeing us:
—I am the other, she said, I am creation
stopped short, not death

as the mother of beauty,
death as the mother.

Eucalyptus Grove

The park is closing; the temporary panic starts
as runners and ornithologists
head toward the gate, and fog
the color of eucalyptus bark

bends low, telling the great trees they can begin
the muffled bray
of saplings rubbing against their elders,
the dolphin-squeal and rusty singing

of a thousand difficult gates in the dark.
It should be easy
to talk as they talk,
not like other trees in the park—

the blunt-hearted willow hugging the streambed,
dropping its lines
like a Chinese poet—
but with the admitted failure of talk.

In this short light, the late-departures see
the delicate attachment
of smoky leaves that fall
in gray apostrophes,

the bumpy rosettes of the pods
with Celtic crosses in the hearts,
the valves that clamp so tight they never
show their peppery black seeds.

It should be easy to talk as they talk, shedding
the false selves by degrees—I used to call them
paint-by-number trees because it looks as though
something is being put on, not taken off—

and it never seemed to matter
to the tree how much it was losing;
the others stood by singing
as the tree would show the glitter underneath.

The great hurt hangs on for a while,
and then reveals the maps
of mauve and rust, the wounds
of a true self no less mysterious.

Canyon

Two fawns in the sun: twin deaths: one
gazes with unbearable steadiness;
the other looks up as the id looks up,
his ears twitching the victory sign;

but oh how close he is
to the beloved, solid so solid on his split hooves;
the wheatgrass rattles gently all around him, dry
as the pages in the rare-book room.

Sometimes you are known completely
by seeing, known as if by a secret companion:
eyes pressed from the base of an incline
into the depths of your perilous being.

> The Tilden helicopter circles the park,
> torso sectioned, like a dragonfly's.
> It hovers a few minutes over the swampy places
> then moves on up to Inspiration Point
> a little haltingly, dragging a sound;
> if it were night, they'd have the searchlight on—
> pale cone spilling far down on the suspect—
> but it is pure, permanent afternoon.
> I'd like to motion them all to come down,
> ask them what it was like in the disjunction;
> does the real grass flatten and the invented
> suspect smile in the invented grass?

Jewel Lake recedes, being drawn off
from the side, and ducks patrol
the strip beside the bench where the mud
dries in an alphabet of C's; I wish

there were more words. A word
for "frightening home." The curve of the hills
against each other, like a lion's paws, and your
intimate recalcitrance on the phone; the quarters

spilled during my aimless speech. I pretended
you were living in another country, not far,
yet impossible to reach, bending over a dirt-brown desk,
revising your manuscripts, and I had rushed out here

to be your opposite—the iron cogs
pushed the elements together, pushed the fog
and the rust—but we were already opposites;
it seemed you were water, and I was the acre of dust . . . .

A flock of bird-watchers blocks the path,
field glasses hanging from their necks;
one has his finger in the book and mutters to his wife.
I need to see my favorites before they spoil
the woods with too much sight:
spatter-bird, hinge-bird, the quail
with the periscope hat. The expert
sets his eyes under the rim for the act
of observation. He must see the yellow shawl, accept
the flash, find the name: oriole.

Then the road lies
like a nerve cell, electrical, thin—
I recall the illustration in the text, how the solitary
impulse, like a hiker, hurried down,

disturbed the obstinate whiteness
of the membrane, climbed
into blockish boats ("receptors"),
was ferried across the synapse, the little

Lethe between two cells . . . .
Things cross this road with greater ease:
bits of mist, those puffy,
hysterical seeds like ions, unchanged

before they disappear. Two walkers
up ahead pass one voice
back and forth, as we do sometimes;
pain lags behind them, holding several spears.

    My great fear
    was not of death but of your great fear
    that you would be on earth without me
    for a long time, perhaps in these hills,
    or between time and place, and I
    because of punishment or belief
    would be conscious only of your inability
    to see the hills in their excellence
    without me, and then, because dead souls
    are nervous, I'd be called away
    as just now the thirsty stag was called away. . . .

Thinking I'd feel nothing
without your hands, their girlish strength (as you
could feel nothing without my boyish ones), I touched
the candelabra flower of the buckeye

where fleshy rose gave way to impure white,
a triumph of repression, the wooden seeds
bursting to a place where thousands of gnats could spawn
and leap, random as electrons;

I sensed as I reached the new colors
they would be retracted any second—like titration
in a chemistry experiment—drop by drop, at some stupid whim;
but the light was changing, and would not change back.

　　The same hard light out here as at that party:
　　you held your glass with two hands,
　　its rim the weighted hoop
　　that angels are required to hold;
　　the guests were ugly as the evening came on,
　　but in their ugliness seemed to lean on one another,
　　archaeological sites at once spectacular and ridiculous.
　　The berries dripped heavily, the apples dripped
　　their ornaments in stairs,
　　you stood among the platters and the lamps, holding
　　daylight there against its will, trapping
　　my vague sentences inside your orderly response . . . .

I bow to the dowager weeds
and they bow back in spiked, fluted collars,
clicking their nails as they shake in the fog;
the party is starting behind them, with castanets . . . .

In the dream, the train with one car only.
We were on some straw the color of the hills,
having a chat,
then the train stopped . . . . The bodies were removed . . . .

　　Over the pods of eucalyptus
　　and the triplets of poison oak,
　　a spider drops down off the lupine stalk,
　　tiny arthritic fingers touching,
　　as I cannot touch, anything at all:

it is neither subject nor object, it has no separate
motions in its realm but lets itself gently down
into the notch and crack of the inexpressible . . . .

We were too thin and awkward,
my hair curled sideways, like a violin;
I hated the corporeal except when it reminded us—
with its jabbing, central pain—how well

the body sees ("vague California mysticism," you said);
I loved the hills because they had no body
but their stumps and fawns,
and they improved in their desolation,

the grasses, turning San Quentin yellow,
and imagined our clarity as a series of white shadows,
fawn's spots, lacunae of the spirit
where our blindness met the blindness of the world.

Plutarch's model of the mind
also has a hill, something like the "life zones"
in the plant book; the normal soul
has an extra soul above it—an invisible friend—
and over the extra soul hovers the divine,
one of the fishbone clouds of Tilden . . . .
I picture you starting your hike
in your inappropriate black shoes, bent as if over
a translation in this foreign light,
or like a wick above a candle . . . .

I can't look too closely at the faces
of runners; they wear their deaths,
working out for the long, local races,
or when they descend the haunted road

after the natural morphine makes of the body
a stem of soothing light, their eyes glaze
with experienced hungers—that need,
when one is running, to blurt out truths

that are not actual truths—
I think about the woman in the cap
who needed water, who staggered like a drunk,
for whom the cheering didn't matter; she said

she didn't know the difference
between the men in lab coats and the finish line,
but with great yearning,
she spoke of the race as of a beloved tormentor.

    Just as, in certain altar paintings,
    the donor stands off to the side, his prayer
    like an insect in his weak blue hands,
    I used to stay outside the house at night;
    the lower honey-colored lights were on
    and it was pleasant to be detached from its
    complex articulations . . . . Of course,
    in those paintings, the holy family never turns—
    Mary's swollen ankles—they keep the donor
    separate like the unconscious, too plain
    for art against the pleated background;
    I stayed a long time like this, apart, and felt
    quite blessed under the brittle stars.

Beyond the gate where you have never been,
and never would be, unless I'd take you there, a thin
rust-colored tree bends over the path—
madroña—its fingers reaching for the hikers;

and if it did not resemble the suicides
in Dante—break one piece off and it speaks—
it would be one Berkeley version of the good life:
self-denial and pleasure; its capillary

branches taper, the frail bark has been gouged
by some fool's pocket knife, and each day
more of its skin is peeling
and sent off like airmail paper.

That night at dinner when you sank
into your gloom (I didn't know you sank until
you told me later) and I was not
your "girl" anymore, still I reached for you

like that red tree: anxious, pure, hard, stubborn fire . . . .

In the hour
of hesitation, in the slanted light,
the fawns come out again
like border guards, and one hides;

your childlike, careful voice
trying to explain the thing too much,
and I squint in the restaurant's poor light,
for this mild calm is not the happiness we envisioned . . . .

We shall know without judgment
in the fullness of time—it says that
in some religion. The brave fawn waits
for its companion, and its spots shine

like spilled quarters in the sun.
The scared one steps into the road at last,
becomes the other one;
then the spotted earth becomes the fawn's back.

Pavane at Dusk

The men have gone off so the women go out to the garden
as if it were war but it isn't,
it is cold summer, the fruit refusing, a fertile
confusion rising in the warrior-heads of the onions,

and such abundance in the shaggy herbs,
in the lettuces, in the rich soil
where the worm turns . . . it wants to be alone,
without oppressive happiness.

The music is the music of failed expectation.
The child scampers around, oblivious,
as the shadows are pulled from her body.
She heaps brown petals on the cold bricks,

and the women talk, steadily, smoothly:
gratifying work, as if a carpenter
were sanding a plank of wood,
they work their sentences of understanding—

but it is too late for this,
the light is dying now,
it is much too late to be understood . . .

Their laps are full of fallen leaves, and light
strikes the fortress with a muffled click . . . .
The child hums, hammering brick, unsteadily—
no, it's the little feudal angel hammering gold.

To the Gull

Does a poem pre-exist
as dawn pre-exists,
as the dagger smelt shine
before being caught,
taking breath into finality?
You wait nearby
with the curved, resentful
nose of medieval peasantry,
your still, disinterested eye
coming straight from the mind
of Dürer, whose grotesques
line the walls at school . . . .
Watching you,
I don't care that my body
will die, for it has not known
its proper freedom,
nor believed the great lie,
that it is good
to be alone;
but you, my beautiful,
stupid, mindless one, have made
your decision against the will,
to go with the inevitable,
tucking your brief
orange legs into your belly.
I have seen you shattered
on the bridge as you landed,
your life lost, have seen
your shallow threes against
the evening sky,
or beside me on the beach,
abandoned in the sand
like an old tennis shoe,

and in the picture
where the girl who has no gift
for flight holds the red
ribbon around your throat
and rides you—
Oh, take me too!
Over the tortured cypresses,
over the freighters stopped like words,
for the spell is broken
and the muse is dead,
do you see his body
on the battered sloop?
Why are you
at the rail again, kelp
caught in your claw, tracing
with your poet's eye another
blinding circle you must fill?

About the author

Brenda Hillman won two awards for her first book of poetry, *White Dress*, a Wesleyan New Poets book published in 1985, the Delmore Schwartz Memorial Award from New York University and the Norma Farber First Book Award from the Poetry Society of America. She received an NEA fellowship to work on *Fortress*, her second book. She teaches writing at St. Mary's College, Moraga, California, and lives in Kensington, on a hill overlooking Berkeley. Hillman is a graduate of Pomona College (B.A. 1973) and of the University of Iowa (M.F.A. 1976).

About the book

Fortress was composed by Marathon Typography Service, Inc. in Durham, North Carolina, on a Mergenthaler Linotron 202 in Palatino, a typeface designed by Hermann Zapf. Since 1938 Hermann Zapf has designed 175 alphabets for hand composition, Linotype, photocomposition, and digital laser systems. Palatino is based on Renaissance forms, and was named after the Italian writing master Giovanbattista Palatino. It was introduced in 1949.

Wesleyan University Press, 1989